Breakthrough Declarations to Receive Money

Daily Affirmations to Attract and Provoke Success, Abundance and Wealth

Dr Julian Businge

Copyright © 2020 Julian Businge

All rights reserved. No part of this publication may be reproduced, distributed, or transmitted in any form or by any means, including photocopying, recording, or any other electronic or mechanical methods, without the prior written permission of the publisher, except in the case of brief quotations embodied in critical reviews and certain other noncommercial uses permitted by copyright law. For permission, write to the publisher at the address below:

Greatness University Publishers
info@greatness-university.com
www.greatness-university.com

ISBN: 978-1-913164-65-2
ISBN-13: 978-1-913164-65-2

DEDICATION

This book is dedicated to my husband and children with whom we walk together in our journey of faith to discover God's will for us. Thank you all for allowing me to make a positive contribution to society. Did you know you are the wind beneath my wings?

CONTENTS

Foreword by Amb Clyde Rivers	vi
Introduction	15
Breakthrough Declarations	19
What is Money?	25
Wealth Attitude	37
Faith	49
The Realm of the Spirit	53
A Mighty God you Serve	57
Receive Money	61
Declarations of your finances	65
Spiritual Renewal	69
Self-defense Prayer Points	79
Praying for Financial Wisdom	87
Thanksgiving Affirmations	91
Declarations for Business Success	95
Conclusion	99

ACKNOWLEDGMENTS

All praise, honor and glory to my Lord Jesus Christ for His richest grace and mercy for the accomplishment of this book. This book has been written from the inspiration of the Holy Spirit.

I also acknowledge the cooperation and support I have received through many individuals from the beginning of my journey as an author. First and foremost, my sincere thanks to my husband Proff. Patrick Businge for his time, support, encouragement and expertise to make this book.

I wish to express my deep gratitude to my children Stella and Eric; you are my eternal treasures in my heart. I pray for you, that when you grow older and are ready to be independent in life, you will carry all the good and positives that you have learned into your own spheres of influence.

To my beautiful mother Mrs. Lucy Sabiiti, my precious siblings, relatives, in laws, pastors and friends, am eternally indebted to you all for being a wonderful inspiration and encouragement and support to me. I am also grateful to Delphia Debra who added meaning to my ideas. God Bless you all.

Breakthrough Declarations to Receive Money

FOREWORD

When I was asked to review this work by Dr. Julian Businge, I was excited, knowing that her commitment to excellence in anything she approaches would yield an outstanding contribution to this subject of prayer and Declarations. I was not disappointed.

This book is truly a game-changer and a must read. Dr. Julian Businge has lived this practice in hear life and it has taken her from a life in Africa to a successful entrepreneur in England. Dr. Julian has won the 2020 World Civility Woman of the Year Entrepreneur Award for England for her skill and expertise in entrepreneurship and helping humanity.

This book will give you the mindset and Principles to start winning today because you understand how to make proper Declarations over your life and situations. The difference between winning and losing is information. Dr. Julian Businge's book has the correct information to make you a winner in all things.

Ambassador Dr Clyde Rivers

World Civility Global spokesman

PREFACE

I was born and grew up in Uganda. I now live in the England with my family. My parents are Mr. and Mrs. Sabiiti Jasi, I thank them for bringing me into this world and doing their very best to raise me to become that which Glorifies God. Thank you for your unconditional love and guidance. My father passed away in 2007, May his Soul rest in Eternal Peace. I know you are proud of me daddy and smiling down on me.

All I am sharing now, I've learnt from reading the word of God (Bible), also by listening to Inspired teachings by great men and women of God all over the world. I have been greatly inspired and I am now applying it in my life and that of my family. With the experiences and evidence as testimonies of Gods wonders, I have got, am now sharing with the world.

Do you know that you can influence what happens in the physical realm of life through your understanding and influence over the unseen realm? Over the years, I learned first-hand the power of Declaring the Word of God over my life. Each day I spend time in God's presence, I pray and Declare over any situation in my life and experience miracles and manifestations of my dreams or desires.

When we Decree something, we are making a Declaration that has the weight of The Kingdom authority behind it. 'Your kingdom come, your will be done, on earth as it is in heaven' (Matt 6:10). Our Decree is prophetic when it is sourced in our Heavenly Father's intention. The Holy Spirit has revealed God's will to us. We then have authority on earth to enforce the Father's plans through the agreement of our own words.

This knowledge changed my entire life and made my life more impactful, more fruitful and more fulfilling. When we spend time with God in prayer, the impossible becomes possible. Mysteries are unveiled hence walking in supernatural power and authority.

A Breakthrough or prophetic Decree is an authoritative 'now' word that unlocks the supernatural and causes a shift to take place.

You will learn to pray and receive answers. You are going to command your deliverance from spiritual attacks, evil dreams, invisible barriers.

You are going to speak into the Spirit atmosphere and command your detained angels of goodness to be released.

The word of God is the indestructible weapon of God in the mouth of the believer to confront the enemy in all battles of life.

"A closed mouth is a closed destiny." As far as God is concerned, your mouth is the answer to your victory and breakthrough in life. Use your tongue prophetically and profitably. The miracles are in your mouth.

Imagine commanding your business to flourish and be successful and it does effortlessly…

Imagine commanding your finances to improve and it obeys.

Stop imagining and apply the principles, revelations and keys in this book that will open a whole new experience of God to you. God's wisdom is in His word and those who discover and apply it experience heaven on earth.

Every thought you think and every word you speak is an affirmation. Why not choose to use only positive words to create a new way of thinking, acting, and feeling?

By praying and Decreeing one day at a time or just by opening this book at random, and understanding the strategy, you're taking the first step toward building a more rewarding life of your dreams.

I know you can do it!

Praying prophetically by the power of Declaration, in the morning, afternoon and night is a top secret to win the battles of each day and accomplish your vision, mission, goals, and assignments for your life.

Learn to shout it loud, prophesy it, announce it, demand it, Decree it, Declare it, because you are a king, and the Almighty God will back you up!

All of us have heard that the believer has authority. This is true. However, even though we have heard so, this authority doesn't seem to be our experience.

Some have tried to use the authority they have but have failed; others do not even know the basis of the authority.

This book will help readers move beyond the self-defeating behaviors like speaking negatively over their lives and have positive mind-sets and embrace the "Awesome" person God designed them to be. From now you will learn to exercise your spiritual authority and Royalty.

I see you victorious!

INTRODUCTION

Prophetic prayer occurs when we pray with insights received from the Holy Spirit. We may receive these insights during prayer or pray about a revelation that has already been received.

We can all pray prophetically. However, a prophetic intercessor is not only equipped with insight from the Holy Spirit, the prophetic intercessor becomes the vessel through whom the Spirit Himself prays.

Do you know that prayers are a powerful way of communicating with God? There are times that we need help to get out of a financial crisis. Or may need to break the chains of debt and poverty.

Are you ready to pray for money or a financial breakthrough? My God truly is a God of abundance. He wants to bless you in your coming in and in your going out. So, don't be anxious or fretful for nothing. God has given us a Spirit of Power and a sound mind.

In the world we live in today, financial breakthrough is one of first prayer requests for most people. We all need money to do one thing or the other. The Bible says money answereth all things. Ecclesiastes10:19

There is nobody that has nothing, no matter how bad or how tight it looks everybody always has something that God can use. It is a lie of the devil to keep you in financial bondage and hardship.

As a principle of financial wealth, understand that there is a supernatural flow to finances. Make sure you are joined to the supernatural flow that produces financial ease. Pride is a hindrance to the divine flow and every man must develop a sensitivity to the divine in their lives.

Every man needs money to pay bills, money to rent a house and to invest in something. You also need money to start in your project or contracts, to support health treatment and recovery of lost investment and many more.

Money problem is universal, but we have the keys today to solve it. It's God's will for his people to prosper and be in health even as their soul prospers. It's not greed to want more money it is your portion.

Debt, unpaid bills, lack of money to give or save. If you're struggling with financial problems, you may feel overwhelmed. Maybe you've prayed for God's help but haven't yet experienced solutions.

I believe today marks the beginning of a new chapter in your life of speaking money into existence.

God has given me spiritual insights during prayer and study on trying to solve financial hardships in my life. This book is my opinion and not Financial Management and not a business opportunity. Now I am passionate about helping others on the same journey.

I've been on the journey and still on, growing stronger and better enjoying testimonies.

Have you heard of people tell you that you can't do that thing for example a teacher tell you that you can never speak in public or never amount to anything? Yes, that's what I mean, it's the actual fuel to lead a higher life and speak to yourself that I can do all things

I believe that God will speak to your heart as you turn these pages and Decree and Declare financial breakthrough, miracle money to come into your life starting from now in Jesus name.

Amen.

BREAKTHROUGH DECLARATIONS

Why I Declare?

What ever you need in this life, is all locked in your mouth, with the help of God you can demand to receive what is due to you in Jesus Name and change your personal world.

The power of life and death is in the tongue, (Proverbs 18:21) and whatever I Declare and speak in God's ears, He will do to me (Numbers 14:28).

"You will also Decree a thing, and it will be established for you; So, light will shine on your ways." (Job 22:28 NKJV)

In James 3, we are told that the tongue is like a rudder of a ship. Just as a rudder determines the direction of a ship our words determine the direction of our life. Begin Declaring God's Word over your life that you may be established by them and experience abundant life and blessings.

Chart the course of your life by Declaring Gods Word. He has promised to "watch over His Word to perform it" (Jeremiah 1:12)

God's Word will accomplish what it is sent to do (Isaiah 55:11)

There are a lot of different things you can choose to say. You can choose to quote great philosophers or the opinions of men, you can choose to speak your own ideas or thoughts, or choose to speak about the facts and circumstances you face OR you can choose to Declare God's Word.

The choice is yours and yours alone. I challenge you to choose to Declare God's Word.

"So shall My word be that goes forth from My mouth; It shall not return to Me void, but it shall accomplish what I please, and it shall prosper in the thing for which I sent it" (Isaiah 55:11).

Insert your own name in these breakthrough scriptures, and Declare the many Blessings that are yours through Christ Jesus...

I DECLARE, I am who the Bible says I am, I can do what the Bible says I can do and will have what the Bible says I can have. In Jesus Name.

I DECLARE, I am the head and not the tail. I will lend to many nations and not borrow. (Deuteronomy 28:13). In Jesus Name.

I DECLARE, Everything I put my hand to do prospers. In Jesus Name

I DECLARE, everything and anything that has been lost or stolen is now being restored. I am pursuing, overtaking and getting back everything the enemy has taken. (Joel 2:25; 1Samuel 30:8). In Jesus Name.

I DECLARE, everything that happens to me or around me is ultimately working together for good in my life because I love God and I am called according to His purpose. (Romans 8:28) In Jesus Name.

I DECLARE that God has given me power to get wealth and the anointing of prosperity which destroys every yoke of poverty in the Name of Jesus Christ.

I DECLARE that my God shall supply every need of mine according to his riches in glory in Christ Jesus.

Every need in my life now bows to the authority of this word. In Jesus Name.

I DECLARE, my faith is a magnet that attracts the blessings of God to me. In Jesus Name.

I DECLARE, God is always doing good things with, in, on, for, through and by me! In Jesus Name.

I DECLARE, I have an unction from the Holy Spirit within me that will reveal, teach, and show me all things pertaining to my life and that which I need to know. In Jesus Name.

I DECLARE, my bank account will always be filled to overflowing and my heart burning with passion, purpose and forward progress. In Jesus Name.

I DECLARE, those who bless me will be blessed and those who curse me shall be cursed. In Jesus Name

I am the seed of Abraham in Christ and an heir according to the promise. In Jesus Name.

Steps to making a Decree.

We are all at different spiritual levels of understanding the word of God and its important that we discus the steps which will teach us, guide us or even remind us of who we are in Christ.

1. Step into your Royal status. To those who believe, he has given them power to become sons and daughters of God. Walk and talk like a Royal. You are a child of the Most High God.

2. Speak in accordance with Gods word and his promises. Always quote the scriptures to back you up. For example, God has given us authority over scorpions and snakes, they cannot harm us. Luke 10:19

3. Align your prayers with scripture. God has given us the name of Jesus whatsoever we ask in His Name shall be given to us. For example, when you are Decreeing, say it's done in Jesus' Name and so shall it be. John 14:13

4. See with the eyes of faith. Believe in your heart that whatever you say will come to pass. Blessed is the man who walks by faith not by sight.

Reasons why Declarations are powerful

- A Decree unlocks the resources of the Kingdom of heaven.
- Words change the atmosphere and environment if used properly. In the Bible Joshua told the sun to stand still until he finished smiting his enemies and it stood still.
- Decrees break opposing powers and shift situations into alignment with God's purposes.
- A Decree removes fear and strengthens your faith.

PRAYER:

Dear Lord, I surrender my financial worries to Your love and care. Guide me with Your wisdom and help me make the changes necessary to live as a blessing to others. In Jesus' Name. Amen

Breakthrough Declarations to Receive Money

WHAT IS MONEY?

According to the dictionary, it's any circulating medium of exchange, including coins, paper money, and demand deposits and paper money currency.

Some people say Money is simply Energy. It brings lots of experiences and a variety of things to us.

Money is fuel to help you get to your destination faster. These are a few ways money is defined.

What is your definition?

These definitions help you to prepare the mind to receive money. Most of us have some issues with money. what we hear about money affects us differently especially when we were young, or simply a negative mindset as adults are some reasons for this.

Example, "Money is the root of all evil" is a statement wrongly attributed to the Bible. The correct statement is "Love of money is the root of all evil". It simply means that if we are greedy about money or give money too much of an importance, then that is bad for us.

Most crimes are committed because the criminals lack money. Marriages are failing because of lack of money.

Many lives are miserable due to lack of money. And the funny thing is that most of us face lack of money due to our attitude towards money.

One way of changing our attitude toward money is by repeating powerful money affirmations. Affirmations attract money. In fact, anything we love and focus on is attracted in our life. Affirming is one way of focusing on money.

We must realize that money is not an end in itself. It is a means to an end. That end can be happiness, joy, freedom, etc.

Money is required not just for survival but also to lead a quality life. Quality life does not necessarily mean luxurious life. It can mean a simple life where all requirements are satisfactorily met and some more.

Money is Good

The way you think about money will determine how much of it you accumulate and your financial independence more than any other factor. Your attitude towards money affects your emotions and your motivations.

The fact is that money is good. It takes money to buy homes, cars, clothes, food and most of the good things in life. Money has an energy of its own and it is largely attracted to people who treat it well.

Money tends to flow towards those people who can

use it in the most productive ways to produce valuable goods and services, and who can invest it to create employment and opportunities that benefit others. At the same time, money flows away from those who use it poorly, or who spend it in non-productive ways.

Affirmations to Manifest Money

- I play the money game to win.
- My intention is to create wealth and abundance
- I create the exact amount of my financial success.
- I admire and model rich and successful people.
- I believe money is important; Money is freedom and makes life more enjoyable.
- I get rich doing what I love.
- I deserve to be rich because I add value to other people's lives.
- I am a generous giver and excellent receiver.
- I am truly grateful for all the money I have now.
- Lucrative opportunities always come my way.
- I am willing to constantly learn and grow.
- My capacity to earn, hold and grow money expands day by day.
- I see God multiplying back to me all of the money that I use, give or circulate in any way, in a never-ending cycle of increase and enjoyment.

- I must become that which I say I am; therefore, I boldly declare, I am Rich. I see it and feel it.
- I am rich in health, happiness, love, success, prosperity and money!
- I am the master of money; I tell money what to do. I call money and money must come. Money must obey me. I am not the servant of money. Money is my loving obedient servant.
- I am divine royalty; I deserve all the Goodness of God.

Inspiring Money Quotes

- The lack of money is the root of all evil. *Mark Twain*
- "Some may say money is the root of all evil but being in poverty is a damn shame!" *Reverend Ike.*
- The best thing you can do for the poor is not be one of them" Reverend Ike
- Money obeys what you believe about it. Money is always obeying your thought about it and your belief about it. *Reverend Ike*
- It's good to have money, but don't let money have you. It's good to possess your possessions, but do not let your possessions possess you.
- Nothing decisive will happen in your life until you really decide. Whatever you have said with conviction will come to pass.

Your Relationship with Money

What is your most joyful memory as a child around money?

I remember as a young girl when my parents gave me money to buy lunch at school, I would feel so excited and I would indeed spend it on buying food but would keep some money to buy a book ,I loved buying kids Bible story books without having to disturb anyone for money.

Your relationship with your money is very individual, emotional and personal. Only you can determine how much time and effort you are willing to devote to it. In addition, only you will reap the benefits or problems that will result from your efforts (or lack thereof).

Imagine the kind of relationship we have with our family members as individuals, how would money feel like or look like? your siblings, child, sister, brother, mother or father? Relating to money is every bit as important as relating to the people you care about.

You need to spend time and effort to understand its implications and to find the proper place for it in your life.

What Type of Money Person Are You?

Establishing a good relationship with money starts with understanding what type of person you are and whether you fall into any of the following categories.

- **Spenders**
  Do you frequently make purchases that are beyond your means? Do you purchase things to make yourself happy? Is there a connection between shopping and your mood? If so, then you can consider yourself a spender.

Spenders tend to accumulate credit card debt because shopping to them is an addiction. Spenders spend money in hopes that material items will bring happiness or provide pain relief.

- **Misers**
  On the other end of the spectrum are the misers. Misers absolutely fear poverty and constantly worry about not having enough money to live.

Misers need to feel in control and are generally uncomfortable with any sort of uncertainty. Ironically, misers fear poverty yet they practically live in it because they spend so little.

- **Haters**
  Money haters absolutely detest money and

what it does to people. They eschew wealth and will often live in deprived and desolate conditions. They will purposely avoid material possessions whenever possible.

- **Seekers**
  They obsess over becoming wealthy. These people put a premium on making a fortune with the belief that it will solve all their problems.

There are usually other inadequacies in their lives that they are trying to make up for with material wealth.

Looking Beyond the Money

No matter what money category you fall into, it's important to look beyond the money and to examine yourself from a scientific perspective and most importantly the spiritual view to obtain deliverance and begin to walk in abundance.

What are you really concerned about? If you are a spender, why do you need so many possessions? If you're a miser, why are you so worried? And for money seekers, why are you constantly chasing money?

Pay close attention to yourself when you are answering these questions and you'll slowly but surely realize some of your hidden insecurities and motivations.

For example, why am I a money chaser? I seek money because I want enough money to buy whatever I want and to be able to provide for my family. You can truly look inside yourself and find the answer.

Healthy Relationship with Money

Margarita Tartakovsky, tells us that "When many of us think health and wellness, we think exercise, nutrient-rich foods, regular check-ups and (hopefully) getting rest. We rarely think money".

But "financial wellness is a component of overall wellness," according to clinical psychologist Joe Lowrance, PsyD. He works with clients to identify problematic behaviours around money and create solutions for a healthier relationship.

"Financial health is having a conscious and purposeful relationship with money that is satisfying and isn't overly stressful".

What Does This Look Like?

Financial health or wellness includes spending money based on your values; having low or reasonable debt; saving money to meet your goals; and having a safety net, such as an emergency fund or insurance.

Our financial relationship today stems from childhood, which is when we develop "money scripts," These are our beliefs about money, which drive our financial behaviours. And usually, we're not even aware of them.

Money scripts are shaped by "direct experiences, family stories, and parental attitudes,".

"Specifically, money avoidance scripts or stories (e.g. 'Money is unimportant,' 'Rich people are greedy'), money worship scripts ('More money will make me happier'), and money status scripts ('Your self-worth equals your net worth') are all associated with poor financial outcomes."

Improving Your Relationship with Money

Fortunately, regardless of the state of your relationship with money, you can take steps to improve it. Here are some suggestions.

1. Shine a spotlight on your subconscious stories

"It is critical to make your unconscious money scripts conscious,".

This way you can begin to challenge your scripts or stories in your subconscious mind that stem from when you were young and change them to improve your financial situation. When your scripts remain unexplored, they can influence your behaviour in negative ways – and, again, very likely without your knowledge. We recommend two practical strategies to explore your scripts /stories further.

Interview family members. Ask your family about their early experiences with money. "Every family has a story around money, and family money scripts all make sense when we know the story."

Recall your earliest money memory. Ask yourself these questions, "What is your most joyful memory around money? What is your most painful money memory? What lessons about money did you learn?"

2. Know thyself.

"Our relationship with money is embedded in our larger sense of self," "Money can serve as an important gateway to a deeper, [fuller] understanding of ourselves."

You can learn more about yourself by paying closer attention to your behaviours around money, then use this knowledge to improve your financial functioning.

For instance, someone who goes to the mall and ends up buying items they don't need might actually be feeling lonely, realizing this can lead them to fulfilling their needs in healthier ways (and saving some cash).

3. Consult reputable resources.

One of the reasons people have a poor relationship with money is misinformation or lack of information, try Reading reputable books which can help. E.g. *The Money Trap* by Ron Gallen; *The Secret Language of Money* by David Krueger.

4. Consult the experts.

If your financial wellness is anything but well, seek professional help. For instance, look for clinicians who specialize in financial psychology. "Asking for help or seeking support is not a sign of weakness or deficiency; it is a sign of wisdom and an act of courage."

PRAYER:

Heavenly Father hive us a new attitude and a new commitment to managing our finances wisely and responsibly. Grant me the patience and tolerance necessary to calm my spirit knowing that You have everything under control. In Jesus' Name, Amen.

Breakthrough Declarations to Receive Money

WEALTH ATTITUDE

Have you ever heard the phrase, "He looks like he has money?" How can someone just look like they have money? Even if you strip away the designer clothes, accessories, and toys, you can often tell when someone has a great deal of money to spend, but how is this possible? When you have a great deal of money, you are not only more secure in your financial life, but you are more secure in all aspects of your life.

You know exactly how much you're worth, and you are both willing and able to spend money wherever you'd like rather than having to scrimp and save.

These traits and habits become natural to someone who has money, and even if you don't have a great deal of money to start with, you can get productive habits and traits into your normal mindset, allowing you to become a money magnet yourself.

Money obeys what you believe about it. Money is always obeying your thought about it, your feelings about it, your belief about it."

It's good to have money, but don't let money have you. It's good to possess your possessions, but do not let your possessions possess you.

"Nothing decisive will happen in your life until you really make a decision."

"Whatever you have said with conviction will come to

pass."

Here are two things you can do immediately to improve your attitude toward money:

First, be perfectly honest to yourself with regard to money and to the amount you want to acquire in life. Pretending that you don't care about money when you really do will only make you unhappy.

Second, begin today to think about all the wonderful things that you could have in your life if you had more money. Then, begin to think of all the things that you could do to increase the amount you ear n and the amount you keep.

The Three Attitudes of Wealth

The Legendry, Jim Rohn said that when he made the decision to turn his economic life around, He had to develop a new attitude as well as new concepts. Here's what he used to say: "I hate to pay my taxes." Mr Shoaf said, "Well, that's one way to live."

I countered, "Doesn't *everybody* hate to pay their taxes?" He said, "No! No! A few of us have gotten way past that once we understood what taxes are. Here's the purpose of taxes in our democratic society.

Taxes are how you care for and feed the goose that lays the golden eggs.

Wouldn't you want to feed the goose that lays the golden eggs?"

How do you feel about feeding the goose? You may think the goose eats too much. That's probably true! But better a fat goose than no goose at all. And the truth is, we *all* eat too much. Don't let one appetite accuse another.

Of course, the government needs to go on a diet. So do most of us. But you still have to care for and feed the goose that lays the golden eggs. The right attitude is so important.

You can start by adopting a whole new attitude. The next time you pay money on an account, put a little note in there that says, "With great delight, I send you this money." Billing agencies don't get many letters like that. What a great scenario.

Your financial picture is improving. You can learn to love to pay your bills.

Think of it as keeping the money in circulation. Think of paying your taxes as feeding the goose that lays the golden eggs. It's all a matter of attitude.

One of the classic Biblical stories of all time describes

a fascinating scenario. Here's my interpretation of that story. One day, Jesus and his disciples were standing by the synagogue treasury watching people as they came by with their offerings. Some people came by and put in big amounts.

Others came by and put in modest amounts. Then a little lady comes by and puts two pennies in the treasury. Jesus said to his disciples, "Look at that! His disciples responded, "Two pennies? What's the big deal?"

Jesus said, "No, you don't understand. She gave more than everybody else." They said, "Two pennies are more than everybody else?" He said, "Yes! Because I'm certain that her two pennies represent most of what she has. And if you give most of what you have, then you've given the most." What a lesson to learn. It's not the amount, it's what it represents that counts. Jesus did not reach into the treasury for this little lady's two pennies.

He did not run after her and say, "Excuse me. My disciples and I decided that you're so pitiful and poor that we're giving you back your two pennies." I'm telling you, that did not happen!

If that had occurred, it would have been highly insulting. She would have rightfully said, "I know my two pennies aren't much, but they represent most of what I have. And you insult me by not letting me contribute what I want to contribute, even if it's only two pennies."

She knew, just as Jesus knew, that everybody has to pay, even if it's only pennies. And whether you start with pennies or dollars or nothing at all, remember the three attitudes of wealth.

Once you begin thinking this way, you're free to create a splendid economic philosophy that will get you up early and keep you up late. It will get you thinking about ways to use your resources to realize your dreams for the future. That's what the road to financial independence is all about.

Command your Money

To command can simply refer to giving orders or exercising your authority.

God has given His people the keys of the Kingdom of Heaven. There is a Power Source who lives within each Spirit-filled believer—the Holy Spirit. We can command our money to locate us through prayer and prophetic Decrees of God's Word.

 God has released to us the Holy Spirit power and authority and given us the keys of access to His children. We can possess our possessions.

Breakthrough Declarations to Receive Money

I had to come to an understanding of the purpose of what we possess. We can possess our money through the present truth of what the Father says we can possess. For example, if you purchase your home or car, you are the owner of that home and car. You are now given the deeds to the home and title to the car. Moreover, you are responsible for the overall care of that vehicle and estate. The home is part of your assets, and you are given the keys of access to the home and car.

Furthermore, you have the authority and right to do what you want to do with those two assets because you are the owner. The keys to the home and car represent authority. No one without the keys have the access; and if they forcefully break into your home or car, they are one, breaking the law, and two, they are trespassers, thieves, and burglars.

The intruders are unauthorized and haven't been given access permission and legal authority to enter. If you lose your own keys and have to break in, and the authorities are called, you will have to prove that you are the home and car owner.

The car title, home deed and keys of access is proof of ownership.

Money is supposed to serve you. You are not supposed to be begging for it, much less looking for it. The way God has ordained it, is that it serves you.

Breakthrough Declarations to Receive Money

Now until you understand that and begin to take your rightful place, you will keep begging, and nothing will happen.

These prayer declarations are power charged by the word of God, believe it, Declare it and begin to see the manifestations! Pray with authority & be serious about it.

- I command my finances, my wealth, my riches, my money to begin to locate me now in Jesus Name
- I command every dead aspect of my finances to be resurrected by the power of the Holy Spirit that resurrected Jesus from the grave.
- My money, my wealth, all of my riches, where are you? I call you from the 4 corners of this world! Come to me now in Jesus Name.
- I am rich like my Father in heaven.
- I am loaded with daily benefits
- I prosper in everything I do in Jesus Name
- The Lord is my Shepherd and I shall NOT want!
- I command my wealth to hear the word of the Lord, begin to work for me now!
- I command my finances to fully cooperate with your plan and purpose God has for it.
- My father deploy my Angels to download success, prosperity, health, wealth, vision,

creativity from the Spirit of God into my life. Psalms 103:20
- I command every individual with a diabolical assignment against me to move out of my sphere of influence in Jesus' Name.
- I command those with divinely ordained assignments to locate me now in Jesus Name.
- I command my money, wherever I go, begin to locate me in the name of Jesus.
- I command every positive door closed against you be opened now by the power in the Name of Jesus!

Declarations to Cause Your Money to Resurrect & Locate You

I DECREE, my season of frustration and failures is over now, and I walk in a season of success and prosperity.

I DECREE, The Lord has given me dominion over all the elements and the works of His Hands.

I DECREE, The Angels are descending and ascending according to the words I speak. Whatever is bound or loosed on earth is already bound or loosed in heaven.

I DECREE, Revelation, healing, deliverance,

salvations, peace, joy, relationships, finances, promotions and resources that have been demonically blocked are being loosed unto me in Jesus Name.

I DECREE & DECLARE, YOU SHALL RECOVER EVERY BLESSINGS OF THE DAY AND NIGHT THE ENEMY STOLE FROM YOU, IN THE NAME OF JESUS CHRIST!!

I DECREE, a mighty supernatural supply like never before comes upon me now in Jesus Name.

I DECREE, people will go out their ways to favor me in the name of Jesus Christ.

I DECREE, supernatural speed on Awaited Miracles, Signs, Wonders, all your Testimonies shall be Delivered unto You without further delay in Jesus name.

I DECREE, a positive financial TURNAROUND in my life now in Jesus Name!

I DECREE and declare, a new season and a fresh anointing to receive more money than I've ever imagined in Jesus Name.

I bind every evil force that would try to capture my destiny, in Jesus Name

I plead the Blood of Jesus over every principality,

power, and ruler of darkness and spiritual wickedness in high places assigned against the purposes of God for my life, my family and my Church, my city, my nation.

Every curse sent against my finances is bound and broken and rendered powerless and sent to Hell fire in Jesus Name.

I displace the luciferins spirit; I bind every false light bearer in Jesus Name. My prayers will disrupt the dark plans of the enemies of my destiny.

PRAYERS:

Lord, I come to You with thanksgiving for all You have given us, and how You have blessed and sustained us for all this time. I lift up to You our finances and thank You for Your Word that promises You will supply all our needs (Philippians 4:19).

I pray You would bless us with Your provision now. Give us wisdom as to how to handle all finances and keep us from making any foolish decisions. Bless our work with success.

Reveal to us how we can earn more and handle our finances more efficiently. Show us where we have spent unwisely and how we can cut back expenses.

In Jesus Name

Amen

FAITH

Faith simply means things hoped for, evidence of things not seen. Hebrews 11:1

Rock solid faith and not waiver in your faith and declarations, don't waiver in believing in Gods promises or you will doubt what you have put in the atmosphere.

God is a speaking being, when the earth had no form and filled with darkness, God spoke the word, He calls those things which be not as if they are.

By faith I prophesy over your life.

I Decree the favor of the Lord shall look for you to bless you with hard currencies in Jesus Name.

I Decree everyone that sees you, those with whom you interact, conduct business with, lead and encounter will favor you!

I DECREE, your network is global and mutually beneficial!

I DECREE, you receive greater financial anointing! You are a walking magnet for financial increase and favor in Jesus Name!

I DECREE, you experience unprecedented breakthroughs, unexplainable success and rise as a global influencer!

I DECREE, The equity in your brand increases in value exponentially!

I DECREE, God grants you innovative ideas and solutions that solve industry and world problems.

I DECREE, your net worth increases daily!

I DECREE, financial breakthrough and increase is happening to you now!

I DECREE, favor is given to you now!

I DECREE, you are ascending into your place of dominion, authority and influence now! Today u will rise, mount up and soar!

I DECREE, you are one person away from your greatest opportunities and breakthrough! They manifest now!

I DECREE the eyes of everyone that sees you and interacts with you favors you!

PRAYERS:

Father, I ask you to give us the blessings of heaven! May the heavens over us be opened! May we be pushed forward, advance, succeed, progress and prosper knowing that all of heavens resources are made available to us on demand. By your Holy Spirit may we courageously lose sight of old shores and launch into the deep!

In Jesus Name. Amen

THE REALM OF THE SPIRIT

Your Words Are Commands in The Realm of The Spirit.

The words we speak in the physical realm move mountains and bend destinies in the spirit realm. Even a simple prayer made in faith causes the hosts of heaven to receive their battle commands and work for your good. When we sing songs of worship and praise to God it's like a precious fragrance in the throne room of God, releasing glory to the King of all kings.

The Spirit-filled believer possesses the ability to bind and loose, permit and prohibit, arrest and release. Heaven will back you up as you flow with the Spirit of God. We can command things to turn around and be better through the spoken word. We can prophesy and speak things into existence. We not only speak things into being through the words of faith, but we can rebuke tempest things that abruptly interrupt our lives. Jesus was on the boat asleep, a sudden storm came out of nowhere, and the disciples were afraid for their lives.

Jesus discerns the motive and intent of the storm and spoke to the winds and the waters and His command was obeyed. Be like Jesus and speak to any life-threatening situation like the storm that came forth and command, "Peace, be still" in Jesus' name.

I Decree, Today God gives me confidence and an unshakable faith to succeed and spite of personal, financial and business setbacks, losses, disappointments and challenges! I choose to praise my way into blessings and breakthrough!

I Decree, your Decade is blessed with unusual supernatural opportunities, breakthrough blessings and divinely orchestrated encounters!

I Decree, you push forward, progress, succeed and prosper! III John 2

I Decree Financial Dominion, Global Influence and Economic Favor over your life now! Whatever you do wherever you work and live you will dominate! Authority is a position of control and influence. Dominion is the right to rule! I decree Favor is positive regard, preference and honor! They are yours!

I Declare, I can do all things through Christ Jesus who strengthen me!

My God shall supply all my needs according to His riches in Glory through Christ Jesus. With God all things are possible!

I Decree, the anointing of the Multiplier is increasing my finances and empowering me to fulfill God's divine mandate for my life.

I Decree, my finances are fruitful and increase in an exponential way!

I Decree, Wealth and riches shall be in my house and I shall never know lack!

I speak Psalm 115:14-15:

The Lord shall increase you more and more, you and your children! Ye are blessed of the Lord which made heaven and earth.

I Decree, nothing shall decrease in your hands. You shall only know increase! You shall know no lack only abundance, progress, favor, success and increase!

I Decree, every word declared in your life on the Altar of God will come to pass in this season.

I Decree, the work of your hands be blessed. Your hands will never be dry.

PRAYERS:

Dear God, shine your infinite light into my life, bless me with abundance so that my family may thrive.

In Jesus Name. Amen

A MIGHTY GOD YOU SERVE

When I was young, there was a familiar saying, "Sticks and stones may break my bones, but words will never hurt me." Stick and stones can break bones, but I beg to differ with the rest of that saying. Words can harm a person, mentally and psychologically. Words have the capacity to hurt feelings, create wars, curses, and even bring about poverty, sickness, disease, and emotional pain. In the natural realm, words can hurt or damage people's feelings. However, in the spiritual realm, words are containers of power that can change your life, alter your destiny, direct your future, and permit you to get your priorities in order with God's will. Words can carry God's supernatural power to heal your body, bring financial breakthrough blessings, and change any circumstance and situation instantly. Words carry the potency of bringing the prophetic promises of the Lord from the spiritual realm into the natural realm.

God has not created you to be poor and broke, sick for the rest of your life. It is not the will of the Lord for you to be like that; rather He came that you may have life. Break every fear, doubt, and personal reservation concerning your financial breakthrough. Oftentimes, we are waiting for the pastor, prophet, to touch and pray for us to receive our deliverance from generational curses. However, it will be your faith that will make you whole.

I Decree today, the Lord is changing the strategy without changing your dreams, in Jesus Name

I Decree divine protection, intervention on every unresolved issue in your life.

I Decree angels are assigned to push back every attack and release blessings to replace burdens.

I Decree you receive divine revelation, visions and prophetic insight the wisdom into diverse strategies, establish actionable goals and the power to cause them to come to pass In Jesus Name.

I Decree every good and perfect gift from above, locates you in Jesus Name.

I Decree, billion-dollar idea, billion-dollar opportunities, wealth, riches, honor, real estate and prime properties manifests now to you In Jesus Name.

I Decree abundance, peace, love and happiness are all yours in Jesus Name. I choose to bear much fruit.

I Decree, the Lord gives you a refund on the unnecessary time I spent and fixes what's trying to break my gift. In Jesus Name.

I Decree, you will succeed in areas u have hitherto failed!

I Decree, Resources and relationships that are needed for your next season, projects, vision, dreams and goals will be made available to you on demand.

I Decree, you will walk in realms of abundance and extreme favor with no lack in any area of your life!

I Decree, your finances come into divine order and are alignment with God's plans to prosper me. In Jesus Name.

I Decree, you are successful enough to leave an inheritance for your children's children.

I Decree Your investments will increase! your health will increase! In Jesus Name.

RECEIVE MONEY

Faith is Heavens currency, in order to receive from God, you must have faith.

Don't speak what you see. Speak what you WANT to see. You can decree and declare over your situation and change it. Right now, as I write, COVID-19 is the talk of the town, we are in lock down and businesses have closed. We have the option to speak fear or speak the word of God. There's always a blessing and opportunity in times of crisis.

Dr Cindy Trimm says "You can order the trajectory of your life and destiny". The ultimate Commander in Chief Jesus Christ the son of God has released delegated authority and power to us the believers. He purposed for us to possess power and authority over the enemy. That may also mean through the power of your commands or declarations. Jesus said we have power over all the power of the enemy!

This means all and any works of the enemy, whether its poverty, lack, fear, sickness, disease, demons' spirits, infirmities, etc. Jesus did not give us power to sit on the sideline and allow the enemy to short cut our healing and breakthrough. Jesus gave us power to do something with it. We possess the same power.

Authority is our heavenly badge, seal, signet, and symbol that represent the government of God through the power of the Holy Spirit. Jesus is the only authority, and everything bows and submits and confesses to Him (Philippians 2:10-11).

Jesus has given us commanding authority over all the works of the enemy, and He supports, backs, and reinforces us.

To Decree means to legislate. And as Kingdom ambassadors, we don't negotiate with life, we legislate. Your words carry power and presence.

Declare these Words over your life and ask God to reveal His Word for you. Because the Devil is afraid of God's Word, but he's even more afraid when you know the revealed Word for you.

I Decree and declare that since, Jesus Christ gave His life as ransom for my sake, I am free from every hold of sin, guilt, shame and death.

I Decree and declare that I will praise the Name of the Lord, all the days of my life.

I Decree My mouth is filled with laughter, and my tongue with songs of joy. And it will be said of me among the nations, that the Lord has done great things for me and I'm filled with joy. (Psalm 126:2-3)

When anxiety is great within me, God's consolation brings me peace. (Psalm 95:19)

Sadness, depression, frustration and every other vice

of the devil is far from me because I have total trust in God, and I depend on Him completely.

I will be still and know that He is God. He will be exalted in all areas of my life. (Psalm 46:10)

I Decree, God will cover me with his feathers, and under His wings will I find refuge; His faithfulness will be my shield and rampart.

I will not fear the terror of night, nor the arrow that flies by day, nor the pestilence that stalks in the darkness, nor the plague that destroys at midday. (Psalm 91)

I Decree God will satisfy me with long life and show me His salvation. (Psalm 91:16)

I Decree and declare that no curse over me can stand because, Christ hath redeemed me from the curse of the law, being made a curse for my sake: therefore, I have dominion over generational and territorial curses. (Gal 3:13)

I Decree and declare that every voice of the devil accusing me is silenced, and every legal access the enemy has into my life is blocked by the blood of Jesus.

I Decree and I declare that I go through life with good and godly friends.

DECLARATIONS FOR YOUR FINANCES

John 1:12 (NIV)

"Yet to all who did receive him, to those who believed in his name, he gave the right to become children of God."

It is God's desire for His people to take possession of what He has given them while knowing their spiritual rights. I believe it is not the Word of God that is the problem, it's our faith to believe what the Word of God says we can possess. The Word of God is true, and it works every time—if we allow it to work. We have to take God at His Word. In other words, we have to possess God's Word and use it for our benefit.

The Word of God is the key, and the Holy Spirit is the compass for healthy, prosperous, and righteous living. We have to know that Jesus' authority lives in us. It is not just any authority in us, it's the only authority in Jesus that is in us.

If you have yielded yourself to sin, prayerlessness and unbelief which has opened the door to Satan and given him legal right to afflict you, then you must repent to God, renounce the act of sin, and close every legal ground given to the enemy. Evict, sever, and shut any evil alliance or open door. In Jesus Name.

Breakthrough Declarations to Receive Money

I Decree and declare that I live in wealth and abundance and I prosper, even as my soul prospers. (3 John 1:2)

I am neither poor nor beggarly.

I have enough and I have in excess.

I call back to my life, every missed good opportunity and I decree that I'm restored.

My gates will always stand open, they will never be shut, day or night, so that people may bring me the wealth of the Nations.

I will drink the milk of Nations and be nursed at royal breasts.

Instead of bronze, I will be brought gold, and silver in place of iron.

No longer will violence be heard in my land, nor ruin or destruction within my borders

The sun will no more be my light by day, nor will the brightness of the moon shine on me, for the Lord will be my everlasting light and glory.

I Decree and declare that my clients and customers prefer me, because my work and business is anointed, and the finger of God is upon me.

I Decree and declare that I am favored of God and of men.

I Decree and declare that I will not borrow rather, I'll lend to nations. (Deut 28:12)

I Decree and declare that nothing dies in my hands

I Decree and declare that this year, God is doing a NEW THING. (Isaiah 43:19) He is making a pathway out of the wasteland for people and is providing streams in the wilderness.

Breakthrough Declarations to Receive Money

SPRITUAL RENEWAL

"I love the LORD, for he heard my voice; he heard my cry for mercy. Because he turned his ear to me, I will call on him as long as I live." Psalm 116:1–2 NIV

I speak the opening of heavenly gates and ancient doors that will bring us into deeper relationship with You, God.

"Lift up your heads, you gate; be lifted up, your ancient doors, that the King of glory may come in." Psalm 24:7 NIV

We decree a time of renewing our strength and soaring in Your Presence God.

"… but those who hope in the LORD will renew their strength. They will soar on wings like eagles; they will run and not grow weary; they will walk and not be faint." Isaiah 40:31 NIV

We declare that the times of spiritual hopelessness and disappointments have come to an end. This is a year of sudden good breaks.

"Unrelenting disappointment leaves you heartsick, but a sudden good break can turn life around." Proverbs 13:12 MSG

Make us ministers of reconciliation to offset injustices and bring healing to people everywhere we go.

"All this is from God, who reconciled us to himself through Christ and gave us the ministry of reconciliation." 2 Corinthians 5:18 NIV

We agree with the new things that will bring spiritual refreshing to those who have been in the wilderness.

"Forget the former things; do not dwell on the past. See, I am doing a new thing! Now it springs up; do you not perceive it? I am making a way in the wilderness and streams in the wasteland." Isaiah 43:18–19 NIV

We declare a new day, as God's light shines on and through us.

"Arise, shine, for your light has come, and the glory of the LORD rises upon you." Isaiah 60:1 NIV

"Enlarge the place of your tent, stretch your tent curtains wide, do not hold back; lengthen your cords, strengthen your stakes." Isaiah 54:2 NIV

Teach us to love, as You love us, God.in Jesus name.

>Amen

Breakthrough Declarations to Receive Money

WARFARE PRAYER POINTS FOR DELIVERANCE

- Father, I thank you for you are indeed my Jehovah Jireh, The God that always provides for me.
- Father release your Fire to consume all satanic agents that are harboring my blessings in the name of Jesus.
- I separate myself from any financial devourer, in the name of Jesus.
- I command the thunder of God to break to pieces all demonic strongmen standing between me and my financial breakthrough, in Jesus' Name.
- I possess all my properties, in the name of Jesus.
- Let all satanic instruments used against my finances be destroyed, in Jesus' Name.
- I command all satanic clearing houses and agents to be roasted, in the name of Jesus.
- I paralyze completely all buying and selling by witches and wizards against my life, in the name of Jesus.
- Let all satanic weapons fashioned against me be disorganized, in the name of Jesus.
- I refuse to be subject to financial failure, in Jesus' name.
- I refuse to do profitless work, in the name of Jesus.
- Every evil force against my handiwork, be destroyed, in the name of Jesus.

- I send back to the sender every arrow of the devil against the fruit of my labor in the name of Jesus.
- I Decree that the works of my hands shall prosper in the name of Jesus.
- I cover my handiwork with the fire of God, in the name of Jesus.
- I cover my handiwork with hot coals of fire, untouchable for evil forces, in the name of Jesus.
- O Lord put to shame every anti prosperity force that is against my handiwork.
- My handiwork receives the touch of the Lord, in Jesus' name.
- Every tree of profitless hard work be uprooted, in Jesus' name.
- You labor of the foolish, pack your load and go out of my life, in the name of Jesus.
- I will not carry any evil load forward in my life, in Jesus' name.
- O Lord drain out satanic deposits from my business and handiwork.
- I release the fire of the Holy Spirit against every strange hand against my business and in the Name of Jesus.
- Let the Spirit of favor fall upon me now, in the Name of Jesus.
- O Lord, enlarge my coast in Jesus name

- I rebuke every devourer in my handiwork, in the Name of Jesus.
- O Lord cause ministering Angels to bring in customers and money into my business.
- I bind every spirit of trial and error, in the Name of Jesus.
- Let every trouble emanating from envious business partners be rendered null and void, in the name of Jesus.
- O Lord, surprise me with abundance in every area of my life.
- I command a quit notice to every evil leg in my finances in the name of Jesus.
- Let the anointing for money-yielding ideas fall upon my life, in the name of Jesus.
- I bind every spirit of fake and useless investment, in Jesus' name.
- I command every effect of strange money on my business to be neutralized, in the Name of Jesus.
- Father Lord let all satanic hosts against my prosperity receive blindness and commotion, in the Name of Jesus.
- All hindrances to my prosperity, be electrocuted, in Jesus' Name.
- Let all my mistakes be converted to miracles and testimonies, in the Name of Jesus.

- I command all those who vow to hinder my prosperity to somersault, become naked and confess to death, in Jesus' Name.
- I command all my buried blessings to come out of the graves, in Jesus' Name.
- Father Lord use both men and women to bless me, in the Name of Jesus.
- I command all my blessings to locate me today, in the Name of Jesus.
- All my blessings attached to my place of birth, be released, in the Name of Jesus.
- Father Lord use all the people in my environment to bless me and let anointing of prosperity fall on me, in the name of Jesus.
- Lord, by the power of the blood, remove from my life any hindrance of the enemy in Jesus Name
- O Lord drive away all forms of lack in every area of my life in Jesus name.
- O Lord, shield me from all forms of deception in Jesus Name
- O Lord, open the eyes of my understanding to see the secret to great wealth in Jesus name

Father, I thank you for answering my prayers in Jesus Name. Amen

Breakthrough Declarations to Receive Money

SELF-DEFENSE PRAYER POINTS

- Let the powers of the wicked be blown away as the chaff before the wind, in the name of Jesus.
- Let the way of the wicked assigned to any area of my life perish, in the name of Jesus.
- O Lord, laugh at all the evil counsellors that are against me to scorn in the Name of Jesus
- O Lord, scatter all the evil men that are gathered for my sake in Jesus Name
- O Lord break the backbones of my enemies with a rod of iron in Jesus Name.
- O Lord, dash my enemies to pieces like a potter's vessel in the name of Jesus
- O Lord, smite all my enemies with all manner of evil plagues in the name of Jesus
- O Lord, break the teeth of the wicked in my life in Jesus Name
- O Lord destroy the enemies using poisonous tongues against my life and destiny in Jesus Name.
- Let all my enemies fall by their own counsels, in the Name of Jesus.
- Let the wicked be cast out in the multitude of their transgression, in the Name of Jesus.
- O Lord let all my enemies be ashamed and be troubled in the Name of Jesus.
- O Lord let all my enemies receive sudden shame and let their arrows return back to them in the name of Jesus.

- O Lord let the wickedness of the wicked come to an end.
- O Lord prepare the instruments of death against my persecutors.
- O Lord ordain Your arrows against my persecutors.
- O Lord let the enemies of my soul fall into the pit which they dug.
- O Lord let the mischief of the oppressors come upon their own heads.
- O Lord, just like you spoke to the earth, and it brought forth all kinds of plants, fruits and seeds, I speak to the works of my hands this day, "bring forth fruits and seeds" in Jesus Name.
- Satan's reign of terror in any area of my life ends now in Jesus Name.
Amen

Breakthrough Declarations to Receive Money

PRAYER AGAINST STAGNATION

2 Timothy 1:6: Revelation 2:1-2: James 1:4

- O Lord, remove me from any work that will endanger my health, give me a work that will bring joy and rest to my soul in Jesus name.
- O Lord remove pain and bitterness from my heart and those with whom I work with in Jesus name.
- O Lord Bless the work of my hands after the order of Abraham, Isaac, and Jacob in Jesus name.
- O Lord cause me to excel in my work, like Jacob by giving me creative ideas to solve complex problems at my place of work in Jesus name.
- O Lord let excellence reflect in my work henceforth in Jesus Name.
- O Lord promote me and my work before those that matter in Jesus Name.
- I prophesy that the rain of hot coals, fire and brimstone and a burning wind shall be the portion of those who want to block my progress at work in Jesus name.
- O Lord let there be restoration of all that I have lost in Jesus name.
- O Lord, by your favor, cause me to sit with people in high place in Jesus name.

Breakthrough Declarations to Receive Money

- O Lord send me my destiny helpers today, those you will use to catapult me from where I am to where I dream to be in Jesus name.
- O Lord! I use my offerings, tithes and kingdom investments as a point of contact for this prayer that in the name of Jesus Christ, let them all come to the remembrance of God so that I receive divine blessings.
- O Lord, I put my trust in you, settle me in the area of my work in Jesus Name.
- Oh Lord, by your unending favor where others fail in their business, let me succeed in Jesus Name.
- O Lord, do not let my mockers prevail against me, settle me in the area of my work and take all the glory in Jesus Name.
- O Lord, by the time I am through with this prayer, let goodness and mercy continually follow me in my place of work in Jesus name.
- Lord, Remove poverty and backwardness from my life in Jesus Name.
- O GOD OF HEAVEN fight the battle of my Destiny and give me victory over all, in Jesus Name.
- I take my work to a green and fertile land today in Jesus name.
- O Lord, I declare today that my work will be moving from one level of profit to another, I

shall never know backwardness and downwardness again in Jesus name.
- O Lord don't let my enemies pull me back to poverty and joblessness in Jesus name.
- O Lord take my work out of a small place to a large place so that my work will expand very fast in Jesus name.
- O Lord deliver my work from trouble waters in Jesus name.
- I Declare that I shall see the marvelous works of God in my place of work in Jesus name.
- O Lord deliver me from the brutal hands of taskmasters at work, by your grace lift me up to become a leader by example in Jesus name.
- O Lord, I declare that the influence of the bad economy of this nation will not affect my work negatively in Jesus Name.
Amen

Breakthrough Declarations to Receive Money

PRAYING FOR FINANCIAL WISDOM

What we learn about money comes mostly from our parents, guardians while growing up. Some are good and others not, these financial habits and scripts become ingrained in us. As adults ourselves now, it takes mental effort to change the way we think about, earn, use, and save money. Allow the Holy Spirit to create in you a new mind about money.

Money can be scary to talk about for many people. We're often afraid of doing the wrong thing with money or making a huge mistake. It can be overwhelming to look at your credit report, have to dispute a credit card charge or tackle a high amount of debt.

Look your fear in the face and arm yourself with the best resource available: education and prayer for without God we can't do anything. Money can be emotional for many. It's something we often tie to our self-worth and self-esteem. Being "good with money" or having money doesn't make you a better person than anyone else.

 Money is a tool that can help us live our best lives and meet our goals. The more you learn about money, the more you can get clear on the goals you have for yourself and reduce your emotional tie to money. No matter what your relationship is with money right now, there is always room for things to become better.

Building Biblical Financial Habits

God Is the Source. Scripture is your invitation to receive God's blessings, act as a wise financial steward of His riches and build a secure financial future. (1 Chron. 29:11-16).

Give to Honor God. Give a Portion of Your Excess to Charity, Tithing, or the act of setting aside one-tenth of your income, is a systematic way of giving. (1 Cor. 16:2) Be encouraged to give back to the society that has housed and helped you get where you are so far. Use Your Capital to Make More Capital.

Live within Your Means. By living within margins, you create space for things to happen.

Make Saving a Priority. Setting aside a percentage of what you earn also is part of stewardship and will allow you to meet planned expenses.

Stay out of Debt. The Bible warns about the risks of going into debt. Although some debt enables you to attain goals, such as a student loan or a mortgage, most debt counters what God wants for you. (Deut. 15:6 and Ecclesiastes 5:5).

Be Content. the common mantra to "use it up, wear it out, make it do or do without" emerged, hence leaving us in debt and fear, worry how to pay. learn how to find contentment in what you have. (Heb.

13:5)

Write It Down. Whether you take pen to paper, use financial planning software or record everything in a financial app, making – and sticking to – a budget allows you to allocate resources efficiently and build a financial plan. (Luke 14:28-30)

Praying for Relief from Debt and Financial Burdens

Lord, I've made financial mistakes. My debts are out of control. But Lord, I know you can open a way where there seems to be no way.

I pray for a financial breakthrough in my life right now! Grow my finances and bestow on me wisdom to manage your blessings righteously. Open my eyes today to job opportunities and profitable business ventures.

May I be good stewards of all that You provide. Help me to not depend on money but only on You, Jehovah Jireh, my Provider. Don't allow money to destroy my relationships through tension and disagreements

I praise You, Oh Mighty King, I bless Your Holy Name. Thank You for providing all my needs, according to Your riches in Glory. In Jesus Name Amen

Breakthrough Declarations to Receive Money

THANKSGIVING AFFIRMATIONS

"Oprah Winfrey attributes much of her success to the power of gratitude—that right there is enough to get anyone to count their blessings. A study from Harvard suggested that expressing thanks could be one of the simplest ways to feel better.

I feel that and I believe it. The more I put a gratitude practice into practice, the more I am convinced that it works wonders on uplifting the spirit and also with manifesting the things I actually want in life (and not what I'm complaining about and inadvertently attracting).

In my experience, gratitude also helps with stress. If I'm feeling overwhelmed or stressed, I change my attention on the things that I am grateful for (even having to do with the situation at hand).

Since, the quality of life is all about perception, the simple shift in consciousness to gratitude makes all the difference. The more grateful I am, the more manifestations and beauty I see around me.

Sometimes a simple affirmation like, "I'm so thankful for my family," can just about get my eyes to water and fill me with immense joy.

Learn to be thankful for what you already have, while you pursue all that you want. —Jim Rohn

If you want to turn your life around, try thankfulness.

It will change your life mightily. Gerald Good.

Gratitude is the sweetest thing in a seeker's life – in all human life. If there is gratitude in your heart, then there will be tremendous sweetness in your eyes. – *Sri Chinmoy*

When you say your affirmations and feel thankfulness deeply in your heart.

Even if some affirmations you make at times don't seem "true" and genuine, still feel it as if it were. This is the power of affirmations /declarations—they bring us closer to what we want /goal by feeling that they're already in our reach / life's truths.

Gratitude Affirmations

- I am so grateful to be alive.
- I am grateful for all the blessings I have.
- I live my life with awareness and gratitude.
- I choose to be thankful no matter my circumstances.
- Life gives me abundant blessings to be grateful for.
- I find something to be grateful for every day.
- I observe the positive flow of life all around me
- The abundance I receive reflects the gratitude I feel
- I am worthy to receive

Breakthrough Declarations to Receive Money

- I am ready to receive
- I see beauty all around me
- I trust myself and accept happiness into my life
- I am thankful for (list 3 things you are truly glad for in your life, can be a person, a thing, a feeling, good news, etc.)
- Yes, thank you.
- I am grateful for all my financial blessings.
- Thank you, God, for your guidance
- I am thankful for the positive relationships in my life
- I have so much to be thankful for
- Thank you for health, vitality, and abundance.
- I am thankful for new beginnings.

DECLARATIONS FOR BUSINESS SUCCESS

Attract your ideal clients

Do you have your own business, or are you thinking about branching out on your own?

Do you want to attract your ideal clients rather than just randomly attracting people who are not a real match for you or your business?

If so, like many entrepreneurs, the topic that's usually on your mind is how to manifest clients in order to be sustainable.

So how can you bring in more clients so that you don't have to worry about how you're going to pay the next bill – or the bill 6 months from now?

The bottom line for our businesses is that we need to make money and for most of us that comes from paying clients/customers.

What I've learned through years of coaching and running my own business is that CLARITY is super important. It's the equivalent of laying strong foundations when building a house.

When you are clear about the sort of clients you want, you become more and more of a match for attracting those clients. Just like you can attract a spouse, so is any area of your life too.

If you feel successful, confident, happy… you become a match for attracting more of the things you want into your business.

I recommend the following strategies to start

- Get clear about who your ideal client is, design your avatar.
- How do you want to feel working with this client?
- How do you want your clients to feel?
- What do you expect from your client?
- If you notice yourself saying "I'm no good at getting clients" you can start using an affirmation saying "I'm a perfect match for my ideal client." and "I'm learning more and more every day about how to reach my ideal clients."
- **My Business Is A Huge Success**
- I believe in myself and trust in my abilities to succeed in all that I do
- Being successful is natural for me
- Success, money and happiness come easily to me
- My work makes a difference
- I am smart and successful
- I can achieve any goals I set myself in business
- I create wonderful business opportunities
- My income is constantly increasing
- My income is rapidly increasing

Breakthrough Declarations to Receive Money

- As I become more and more successful, I help more and more people
- I am passionate about my business and that shows in everything I do
- I easily attract sales
- I easily attract my ideal clients
- My business allows me to have a life I love
- I'm energized in my business
- I love the freedom my business provides for me
- My business dreams are constantly manifesting
- I am a perfect match for my ideal business
- I am thankful for the opportunities that come my way every day and I choose to seize them.
- I am thankful for every person who contributes to the success of my business.

CONCLUSION

Do you realize how much power resides in your mouth? In life it is vital that we understand the power of our words. Our words create our world. Every day we wake up, we have the power to command our lives, remember we are the captain of our ship. You possess so much power inside of you to truly create the life you desire.

When we know what we know, we tend to operate in confidence. When you understand the power, you possess by declaring it daily little by little you will begin to create a life of power.

This book is a powerful tool helping people discard limiting subconscious beliefs and to cultivate positive, empowering beliefs. According to your faith, shall it be done to you. – Matthew 9:29.

I believe, Father, that You wish above all things that I prosper and be in health even as my soul prospers. I will meditate in Your WORD day and night, not letting it depart from my mouth, keeping it in the midst of my heart, observing to do all that is written therein. In Jesus Name. Amen

Remember: The prayers you just made; all the elements heard you. From the four corners of the earth to the heavens. So just begin to thank God that your money is locating you even as you pray. Thank God because you know He is also working on your behalf in Jesus name! Amen.

ABOUT THE AUTHOR

Dr Julian Businge is the Co-Founder of World Greatness Awards. She is also the Founder of Peace Property Education, a firm that specialises in serviced accommodation commonly known as Airbnb. Through this firm, she offers mentoring and coaching services to women looking for time and financial freedom.

Together with her husband, co-founded Peace Apartments in 2016 which operates short term accommodation the London suburb of Luton, UK. Dr Julian Businge is also a Royal Fashions Expert who is creative, caring and customer focused. Her project in 2019 has been working closely with the Queen Mother and HRM King Oyo of Tooro in Uganda to create Royal fashions and design which blends traditional and modern wear.

Dr Julian Businge is a published author, a Representative to the United Nations, and the host of weekly The Success Show on Luton Urban Radio.

Dr Julian Businge won the World Civility Woman of the year entrepreneur Award 2020 UK

Mission

I am on a mission to help as many people as possible to manifest their dreams through obtaining knowledge and belief that what they want /dream can be achieved and live a balanced life.

I live to serve God and serve people.

Purpose

To help people become Empowered and inspired to Live more, be more and WIN more in the most important game you will ever play in… YOUR LIFE!

Vision

To live a life of courage, creative expression, awareness and abundant possibility through clear, compassionate love and service

Social Media Links

joliejasi@gmail.com

https://twitter.com/BusingeJulian

https://www.instagram.com/juliajasi/

TEL: +441582806116

GIVING BACK

Blessed Hill Children's Centre Uganda

It is an organization designed to support, educate, feed and house orphaned, abandoned and rejected children in Uganda. Nearly every year, I get the chance to visit this orphanage and I have witnessed their daily struggles. My dream is to support this orphanage by establishing a bakery which will enable children to learn the life skill of baking. It is my hope that this will promote their economic independence and empowerment for when they leave the orphanage.

If you wish to discuss this opportunity further, please email and together we can make a difference to the orphans living in Uganda. My email is joliejasi@gmail.com

What Now?

Seek a close relationship with the God of the Bible through the Lord Jesus. Dear Lord Jesus, thank you for dying on the cross for my sin. Please forgive me. Come into my life. I receive You as my Lord and Savior. Now, help me to live for you the rest of this life. In the name of Jesus, I pray. Amen.

Don't underestimate the power of implementing the word of God, it's a double-Edged sword, very powerful that will cause results in your life.

Keep in touch with us through social media, website. hearing your feedback, testimonies, experiences from you would make my day fabulous and help me serve you better. In this way, you will also stay informed of what we are up to, events around the world.

Do something nice for someone else by giving them a copy of this book. If someone you know is having financial challenges and needs to learn to do things the right way, get them a copy.

Re read this book in about six months. Change takes time and requires persistence. Go to your calendar now and make this note six months from today. It takes a decision to rewrite the future of your life.

Other Books by Dr Julian Businge

www.ingramcontent.com/pod-product-compliance
Lightning Source LLC
Chambersburg PA
CBHW042337150426
43195CB00001B/21